Terrific Trunks

Columbus, OH • Chicago, IL • Redmond, WA

The McGraw-Hill Companies

The Independent Reading Books

The ***Independent Reading Books*** are reading books that fill the need for easy-to-read stories for the primary grades. The appeal of these stories will encourage independent reading at the early grade levels.

The stories focus on the Dolch 220 Basic Sight Vocabulary and the 95 Common Nouns. Beyond these lists, the books use about three new words per page.

This series was prepared under the direction and supervision of Edward W. Dolch, Ph.D.

This revision was prepared under the direction and supervision of Eleanor Dolch LaRoy and the Dolch Family Trust.

SRAonline.com

 SRA

Send all inquiries to:
SRA/McGraw-Hill
8787 Orion Place
Columbus, OH 43240-4027

Printed in the United States of America.

ISBN 0-07-602517-9

3 4 5 6 7 8 9 BSF 12 11 10 09 08 07 06 05

Table of Contents

Jumbo

You know that anything called "jumbo" is something big, like jumbo peanuts. But do you know that Jumbo was the biggest elephant that ever came to the United States?

Jumbo lived in Africa when he was a baby elephant. He went to live in a zoo in Paris, France. No one at the zoo thought this little elephant was ever going to grow up to be the biggest and best-known elephant in the world.

When the baby elephant was older, he went to live in a zoo in London, England. The manager of the zoo in Paris had wanted one of the animals that lived in the London Zoo. So the manager of the London Zoo gave the zoo in Paris an animal, and the London Zoo got Jumbo. He lived there for a long time. Jumbo was the biggest elephant in the zoo. He was over ten feet high. He was very big and very strong.

Jumbo let the children ride in a big *howdah*, or chair, that was put on his back. The king and queen of England had taken a ride in the howdah on Jumbo. Everyone liked to ride in the howdah. The children of London thought of him as their very own elephant.

The manager of the London Zoo found that on some days Jumbo was not very good. The manager was afraid Jumbo might be a bad elephant. The manager knew that because Jumbo was so big and strong, he could not be stopped if he was bad. The manager was afraid Jumbo might hurt some of the children who came to the zoo.

For a long time Mr. Barnum, who owned a circus in the United States, had wanted to buy Jumbo. Mr. Barnum had many elephants in his circus. If he could buy Jumbo, his circus would have a bigger elephant than any other circus. The manager of the London Zoo thought

Jumbo might be happy in a circus with many other elephants and that he might not get to be a bad elephant, so he sold Jumbo to Mr. Barnum.

Jumbo was an African elephant. An African elephant is not like an elephant from India. African elephants are not used much in circuses. When Jumbo got to the United States, many things happened.

Jumbo Goes to the United States

When the time came for Jumbo to go to the United States, the manager of the London Zoo and the American bull-keeper who was to take Jumbo to the United States tried to get Jumbo into a big open box. But Jumbo just got down on the ground, and no one could make him move.

Then a newspaper in London said, "Jumbo does not want to go to America. He lays down on the ground and will not move. Jumbo loves the children of London. He likes them to ride in the howdah on his back. Jumbo does not want to go away from the children of London."

The children of London sent letters to the newspaper.

Please do not let our big elephant go away.
We love Jumbo.
We want to keep him in the London Zoo.
Patricia Smith

The newspapers in America ran the story about the big elephant that did not want to go away from the children of London.

Mr. Barnum, who owned the circus in America, was very happy about all this. He wanted all the people in the United States to know he had the biggest elephant in his circus.

The children of the United States sent letters to the newspaper in London.

We want to see the big elephant. Please send Jumbo to America.

The king and queen of England did not want Jumbo to go away. They thought the children of England must have Jumbo in the London Zoo.

Mr. Barnum sent a letter to the London newspaper.

We know that the children of London love Jumbo, but the children in America want to see the big elephant. And the children of America will love Jumbo too. After a time I will bring my circus to England. Then the children of London must be sure to come and see "the biggest circus in the world." And there they will see Jumbo.

The English manager and the American bull-keeper tried again to get Jumbo into the big box to go to America. This time they put the big box on wheels, like a wagon. Some of the wagon was in the ground. The big box was open like a bridge. They wanted Jumbo to start to eat on this bridge.

Little by little, Jumbo started to walk onto the bridge and eat. One day, when Jumbo was on the bridge eating, the big box was pulled up around him. Jumbo was in the box.

The big box, which was on the wagon, was pulled out of the ground. Many big horses pulled the wagon down the road to the ship that would take Jumbo to the United States.

People came to say good-bye to Jumbo because Jumbo was the king of the elephants.

The big box was put on the ship for the United States. An English man from the zoo and the American bull-keeper were with Jumbo all the time. When the ship got to the United States, many people went to the ship to get a first look at Jumbo.

The big box with wheels was taken off the boat. Many horses pulled Jumbo, who was in the big box, through the streets of New York City. A band in a wagon played music.

At first Jumbo was afraid of the noise, the people, and the horses on the streets of New York City. But he got used to everything and was a good circus elephant.

The bull-keepers taught Jumbo many things. They taught him to walk at the head of the parade. There is an old picture that shows Jumbo reaching his trunk up to a window at the top of a house. He is eating a peanut from a boy's hand in the window.

Many, many people went to the biggest circus in the world to see the biggest elephant in the world.

A Book about Elephants

Erica, Leon, and Emily were working on a book of photos about elephants in India. They used a big car to get to a river where elephants would drink water. They put the car under some big trees so the elephants would not see it. Then Erica, Leon, and Emily walked to the grasses by the river and watched for elephants.

Soon a big elephant came to the river. Erica and Emily started to take photos. The big elephant looked all around, then it walked into the river. There the big elephant had a little drink of the water from the river and then a big drink.

Did the elephant see Erica, Leon, and Emily? They did not think so.

The big elephant walked out of the river into some trees. Soon it came back and many elephants came with it.

Erica, Leon, and Emily watched and watched. They saw that the big one was the leader of the elephants.

Elephants live in a herd, and a herd has a leader. She watches over the herd and takes it to find water. So when the leader walked back into the river, the elephants did too. Soon all the elephants walked into the river.

The leader looked to see that all was good around the river and that the water was good to drink. The leader did not want any elephants to be hurt at the river.

In the river, the elephants started to drink the water. Leon had some paper. He started to write about how the elephants used their trunks to get water. Erica and Emily started to take photos again to show how the elephants used their trunks to get water.

Erica, Leon, and Emily had waited days to see elephants. Leon had waited days to write about elephants. Erica and Emily had waited days to take photos of elephants.

14

Now the three friends waited to see what the elephants were going to do. There were many elephants in the river. Baby elephants were drinking and playing with their mothers. The leader waited by the river and watched to see that all was well.

Once, one of the baby elephants went under the water. Emily, Leon, and Erica waited to see if any elephant saw the baby elephant go under. The leader saw it!

The leader went into the water and pulled the baby out of the river. The baby elephant ate some grass and then walked back into the water but not too far.

Leon had to write that down. Erica and Emily had to take pictures of the baby. This was going to be a good book.

Erica and Emily took many photos. They took some good photos of elephants drinking and playing. Best of all were the photos they took of mother elephants washing baby elephants.

The mother elephants would teach the baby elephants what to do in the water. The mothers would teach the baby elephants to draw water into their trunks, and they would teach them to look under the water with their eyes open.

Soon the elephants were leaving the river. They walked back into the trees. The baby elephants walked by their mothers. The father elephants went into the trees after the mother elephants and the baby elephants.

As the big leader was leaving, it looked right at the three friends. The leader looked like it was going to stop. Emily took a photo of it looking at them. It was a good photo.

The friends waited to see what the leader would do. The leader walked into the trees with the elephants. Emily and Erica took photos of the elephants leaving.

Emily, Leon, and Erica did not know what to do now. The friends wanted to take photos and write about the elephants. Could the friends walk into the trees after the elephants?

Erica, Leon, and Emily did just that. But as they did, the leader stopped and looked at them again. The three friends stopped too. The leader put its big trunk over its head.

Emily, Leon, and Erica did not know what the elephant was telling them. Erica took a picture. The elephant stopped putting its trunk up over its head and walked away. Erica, Leon, and Emily did not go after it. They went back to their car.

As they started to go to the car, Emily took photos of the trees and the river. Leon had to write down all they had seen.

In the car, the three friends said much about the elephants and their leader. Now the friends knew that the leader had seen them from the start. The leader knew they could not hurt the elephants, so it did not run at them to make them go away. But the leader did not want the friends to go into the trees after the elephants. That is why the leader stopped them.

The friends knew, too, that they had many good pictures. Leon read what he had written about the elephants. Emily and Erica said that what Leon had written was very good. They liked best what he had written about the big leader.

Soon Erica, Leon, and Emily were far from the trees and the river. They called some friends in the United States to tell them about the elephants. Erica and Emily said they had many, many good photos for the book. Leon said he had written much about elephants in India.

Erica, Leon, and Emily took a big airplane back to the United States. When they got to Chicago, they worked on the book.

Erica and Emily picked the best photos for the book. There were so many good ones.

Leon had to write about the elephants and their leader, the river and the trees, and about Erica and Emily. He would write again and again to make the book just right.

When the book was done, Erica, Leon and Emily showed it to everyone they knew. Everyone who saw the book liked it. Everyone wanted to buy the book.

Soon the elephant book was in stores all over the United States. Everyone knew about the elephants at the river in India. Everyone knew about Erica, Leon, and Emily.

The Flies and the Brooms

It was a very hot day. The elephants in the circus were doing their tricks, but they were very hot and not doing well. The elephants were not happy. They were moving their feet and their tails and their big ears, but they were not doing their tricks. At last, the bull-keeper stopped.

Flies were everywhere, and if there is one thing elephants don't like, it is flies. Elephants cannot get flies off their backs. An elephant's trunk will not reach over its back. An elephant's tail is not long, so it cannot get the flies off its back.

Wild elephants use mud to keep the flies away. But in the circus, elephants cannot use mud to get away from the flies.

A woman who sold toys and peanuts at the circus stopped by the elephants. She had many toy brooms. These brooms were to be sold to the children at the circus.

The leader of the elephants put its trunk up and made a big noise. Then it went over to the woman with the brooms and put its trunk around her. The woman called to the bull-keeper to make the elephant go away, but the big elephant would not go away. The leader of the elephants made a noise with its trunk again.

The bull-keeper knew that the big elephant was trying to tell him something. At first he did not know what it was. Then he laughed.

"I think the elephant wants one of your toy brooms," said the bull-keeper, and he had to buy one of the brooms and give it to the elephant.

The elephant took the broom in its trunk and reached over its back. With the broom, the elephant could reach its back and get the flies off.

Then all of the other elephants put their trunks up and made a great noise. The bull-keeper had to buy a broom for each elephant.

All day long the elephants had their brooms. They paraded through the streets of the city, each elephant holding its toy broom. They did their tricks in the circus, each holding its toy broom. When night came and the flies went to sleep, the elephants put down their brooms.

I think those elephants were pretty smart. Don't you?

The Wild Elephant

A mother elephant had a baby elephant. The baby elephant was a boy. The mother elephant called him Albert.

Mother elephants worry about baby elephants. But if the baby is a boy, elephant mothers worry and worry. Some elephant boys could grow up too wild to live with their mothers or with any elephants. These wild elephants had to live far off in the woods, far from their mothers.

This mother was thinking that her baby boy would grow up too wild. She was thinking that he would have to live far off in the woods. That is why she called her baby Albert. Wild elephants are never called Albert!

When Albert was a baby elephant, he did not look very wild. Albert would always hide under his mother when other elephants came around.

But as Albert started to grow, he liked to play with other elephants like his friends Tina and Waldo. Tina, Waldo, and Albert would run and hide in the woods, but not too far in the woods. They would always hide where their mothers and other big elephants could see them.

As Albert, Tina, and Waldo grew, they grew stronger. As Albert, Tina, and Waldo grew, they ran faster too. But Albert was always stronger and always ran faster. Soon no elephant was stronger or could run faster than Albert.

But Albert could not stop! When Albert ran fast, he could not stop fast! So Albert ran into trees, rivers, and other elephants.

His mother and his friends Tina and Waldo knew that Albert did not try to run into elephants. He just could not stop. But some other elephants did not know that. They started to think that Albert was a wild elephant!

Once, Albert, Tina, and Waldo ran very fast in the woods. Albert saw an older elephant, Minnie, walking in the woods.

Albert saw Minnie before Tina and Waldo saw her. "Stop," he shouted to his friends. They could stop, but Albert could not. He ran into Minnie and knocked her down.

"Help," shouted the fallen elephant. "A wild elephant knocked me down."

The other elephants ran to help Minnie. Many of them shouted at Albert, "You are a wild elephant! You knocked Minnie down."

The leader of the elephants came to see Minnie and Albert. The leader looked at Minnie and saw that she had fallen. The leader looked at Albert. Some elephants had said that Albert was wild. Now the leader was thinking that Albert would hurt other elephants.

"Albert, you are a wild elephant. You must go live far off in the woods, away from all other elephants," said the leader.

Sad Albert wanted to hide under his mother again, like he did when he was little. He asked the leader if could go see his mother before he went to live far off in the woods.

"No, you must go now," said the leader.

Sad Albert walked far into the woods. His sad friends Tina and Waldo watched him go.

His mother, Tina, and Waldo did not see Albert for many years, but he saw them. From far off in the woods, he watched the elephants. Over the years he watched his mother grow older. He watched Tina and Waldo grow up.

Over the years Albert grew up too. He was stronger and faster, and he could stop now! Albert did not think he would knock down any elephants again.

After many years, Albert was on a hill that looked over some woods. He saw the elephants, his mother, Tina, and Waldo. Tina was the leader of the elephants now.

By the river in the woods, Albert saw two other elephants. They did not live with his friends. The two elephants were big, big wild elephants. They ran at Tina, Waldo, and his mother. The elephants ran fast. They were going to knock down Albert's friends and his mother!

As fast as Albert could, he ran down the hill. He ran into one wild elephant—bang—and knocked him down. He ran into the other wild elephant—bang—and knocked him down! Before Albert could bang them again, the two elephants got up and ran away, for good.

"Albert! It is you!" Tina shouted.

"Albert, my boy," said his mother.

"You were never a wild elephant. You just could not stop," said Tina. "As leader, I say you shall live with us from now on!"

Albert looked at his mother, Tina, Waldo, and the other elephants. Albert knew he would never be sad again.

A Tusker Looks after His Rider

Everyone must think. You have to think about things around you. You have to think about what is the best thing to do. It is the way you think that makes you who you are. Elephants can think too.

Some elephants and their riders were helping make a bridge over a river. The bridge was just about finished. There were only three big logs that had to be lifted up to finish the bridge.

A big tusker, an elephant with tusks, who had its rider on its head, was going to put the last three logs on the bridge. It was time to eat, and the rider wanted to get the work finished.

The rider wanted the tusker to pick up the log with its tusks, hold it with its trunk, then lift its head high, and use its trunk to put the log on the bridge.

But the big elephant was afraid to do what the rider wanted. Its rider was on its head, and the elephant could tell that when it lifted its head high, the big log was going to roll back on the rider. It knew the log was so big that it could not hold the log with its trunk.

The tusker loved its rider. If the log rolled back, the rider would be hurt. So the tusker put down the log.

Then the tusker looked all around the ground. Its rider did not know what it was doing. At last the tusker found what it wanted. It was a piece of wood.

The big elephant picked up the piece of wood with its trunk and put the wood between its tusks. When the elephant picked up the big log with its tusks and lifted its head, the log could not roll back on the rider because the piece of wood would not let it.

One at a time the big tusker lifted the last three logs onto the bridge. Then, with its trunk it put down the piece of wood that was between its tusks. Now it was time to eat. And I know that the big tusker was given something very good to eat that night.

Tusko Helps Himself

The Great Tusko was in the Barnes Circus. Tusko was not trained to work with other elephants because he did not always like other elephants. He walked at the head of the circus parade with his bull-keeper riding on his head.

Everyone knew about the Great Tusko. Everyone wanted to see the "biggest elephant in America." Tusko was the biggest elephant then.

The bull-keeper had to watch Tusko. The bull-keeper never knew what would make Tusko angry. When Tusko was walking at the head of the parade, he was always with Ruth.

Ruth was a strong elephant and a good elephant. If Tusko tried to run away, Ruth would always stop him.

There was always a bull-keeper by Tusko because no one knew what Tusko might do.

One day the elephants were going back to the circus after the parade. Tusko was walking with Ruth. His bull-keeper was walking beside Ruth.

All at once Tusko stopped. He saw a man with a big basket of hot dogs. Tusko thought he would like some. He picked up the hot dogs with his trunk. He ate the hot dogs as fast as he could because he knew he was being bad. Tusko knew his bull-keeper would stop him.

The man with the hot dogs shouted and tried to make the big elephant go away. It was a good thing that the bull-keeper was there. If Tusko got angry with the hot dog man, Tusko might have hurt him. The circus gave the man money for his hot dogs.

The circus had to give money for many things Tusko did. But Tusko was a very smart elephant. Sometimes he got angry, but sometimes he was very good and helped his bull-keeper.

Once Tusko was riding in a wagon that was being pulled by a truck. This was not good for Tusko because the wagon moved much. Then the truck turned too fast. Tusko fell over, and the wagon fell over too. One of Tusko's feet got hurt when the wagon fell over.

Now how would you get a big elephant out of an overturned wagon?

The bull-keeper went over to Tusko and said, "Big boy, I am going to help you get out of this, but you are going to have to help me."

The bull-keeper got into the overturned wagon. He got under Tusko's big feet. If Tusko had moved at all, he would have hurt the bull-keeper. But Tusko lay still. The bull-keeper made Tusko's foot better with some bandages. Then he got him out of the overturned wagon.

Tusko stood still while the bull-keeper
got the wagon up. Then Tusko got back
into the wagon. He knew that his bull-
keeper would take care of him.

Elephant Differences

Freedom Zoo is a zoo where animals can run and run. There is a long road in the zoo. A bus takes people around to see the animals. The people must sit in the bus and watch the animals run around. The animals cannot get hurt because they cannot get to the road.

In Freedom Zoo there is an area for elephants. It is a very big area and many elephants live there. Walter and Lillian are two very big elephants that live in the elephant area.

When people on the bus see the elephants, they see Lillian first. They think Lillian is big. But then they see Walter. All the people on the bus say Walter is the biggest elephant they have ever seen! He is very, very big.

Cheryl Banks works at the zoo. She is a zookeeper. She takes care of the elephants in the elephant area. She tells the people who come there all about the elephants.

Once, Cheryl Banks, the zookeeper, was telling some school children about Walter and Lillian. She said, "When people come to the elephant area, they see Lillian first, and they say she is big. Then they see Walter. Then they say they have never seen an elephant Walter's size.

"Well, Walter and Lillian are both elephants, and they look like each other, but they are different. They are not just

different in size but in many other things too!" said Cheryl. "And I would like to tell you about some of those other things."

Just then Walter and Lillian started to walk up to where the children were. The elephants were walking together.

One little girl asked the zookeeper, "It looks like Walter and Lillian are friends. Are they friends?"

"Why, yes," said Cheryl, "they are friends. They are very good friends. They like to walk and run together in the trees and grasses here in Freedom Zoo."

The zookeeper looked at the two elephants and said, "Yes, Walter and Lillian are good friends. They look like each other, but they are different.

"Look," Cheryl said, "Look at Lillian's feet. How many toenails does she have?"

The little girl said, "She has five toenails on each of her two front feet and four toenails on each of her back feet. That's funny!"

"That is right. She does!" said the zookeeper. "Now," she said, "Look at Walter. How many toenails does he have?"

A boy said, "Why, he has four toenails on his front feet and three toenails on his back feet!"

"That is right. He does! Walter and Lillian have different-looking feet," said Cheryl, "but people do not always see that."

Someone said, "No, they do not always see that! What are some other things about the elephants that people do not always see?"

Cheryl said, "Well, look at their tusks. Do you think they look different?"

A girl who was looking at the elephants, said, "Yes, I think they do. I think Lillian's tusks are small, and Walter's tusks are big."

"You are right. Her tusks are small, and his tusks are big," said Cheryl. "You children have very good eyes."

One small boy said, "I can see that Lillian's ears are small, and Walter's ears are big."

"Yes, her ears are smaller," said Cheryl Banks. Just then, Walter moved his big ears from front to back. The children laughed, and so did the zookeeper.

"I can see a difference!" said one of the children. "Look at the top of Lillian's back. Walter's back is not as round as Lillian's."

"Good! You saw that," said the zookeeper. "Now let's look at them again."

"I see a difference too!" said two girls at once. They walked over to Cheryl. One said, "It's their trunks. Their trunks are different!"

The zookeeper said, "Yes, their trunks are different. Walter's trunk has many rings."

Cheryl Banks said, "At first I said these two elephants are like each other, but then I said they are different too.

"Now I will tell you why these two elephants are different. It is because they come from different places. Lillian is from Asia, and elephants from Asia look like her," Cheryl said. "Walter is from Africa, and elephants from Africa look like him."

The children were thinking about this when all at once someone said, "That's just like people. We come from different places, and we are like each other, but we are different too."

"That is right," said the zookeeper. "Elephants are like people. They come from different places. They are like each other, but they are different too."

Cheryl Banks said, "It is good that you know many things about the animals in the zoo. Now you know much about elephants. When you come to the zoo again, you will see the differences in the elephants that many people will not."

Ellie and Gail

Ellie walked in the grass to where her mother was. "Mother, Mother," Ellie said. "I have a new friend."

Ellie was so happy to have a new friend. Ellie was the little elephant in her family. She always did things with her mother and father. She liked doing things with them, but she wanted to do things with a friend too. Ellie wanted a friend!

"Good. I knew you would make friends soon," said Mother. "Tell me all about this new friend of yours."

"She is called Gail," said Ellie. "We play under the big tree by the squirrel's house. She is the little one in her family too! She likes to play under the big tree just as I do. As soon as we started to play, we knew that we would be friends."

"Well, it looks like you and Gail are friends. You are the little one, and so is she. You like to play under the big tree, and so does she. Why don't you have her over for dinner? Then we can all get to know her," said Mother.

Ellie was so happy. She ran to the big tree by the squirrel's house to ask Gail to come over for dinner.

"You can eat dinner with us," said Ellie. "My family gets the best grass from up on the hill and the best water to drink."

"Do you think your family will like me?" asked Gail.

"Yes, they will like you," said Ellie. "You and I are friends."

Gail ran up Ellie's trunk. Then the friends went to see Ellie's family.

Ellie's mother and father did not see Gail right away. Then Ellie lifted her trunk. "Mother and Father, this is Gail," Ellie said.

Ellie's mother and father looked at Gail. Gail was not like Ellie at all! "A mouse!" shouted Ellie's mother.

Ellie's mother and father ran away as fast as they could. Gail and Ellie were sad. They did not know why Ellie's mother and father ran away.

"Let's go to dinner at my house," said Gail. "My family is eating dinner now."

So Gail and Ellie went to see Gail's family. Gail got to ride on Ellie's trunk again. But when they got to Gail's house, Gail's family took one look at Ellie and shouted, "An elephant!" They ran away as fast as they could.

"Why did they run away too?" asked Ellie. "I will go back and tell my family that they must get to know you."

"I will tell my family that too," said Gail.

Ellie went to her family. "Mother and Father, if you would just get to know Gail, I know you would like her," said Ellie.

"But Gail is a mouse!" said Mother. "An elephant cannot like a mouse."

"But I am an elephant," said Ellie. "And I like Gail, and she is a mouse."

Gail went to talk to her family too. "Mother and Father, if you would just get to know Ellie, I know you would like her," said Gail.

"But Ellie is an elephant!" said Mother. "A mouse cannot like a elephant."

"But I am a mouse," said Gail. "And I like Ellie, and she is an elephant." Ellie went back to the big tree. Gail was there.

"It is no use," said Gail. "My family is afraid of you."

"My family is afraid of you too," said Ellie.

"Well, what can we do?" said Ellie.

"Well, we could stop being friends," said Gail.

"But we like to play with each other," said Ellie.

Just then Ellie's mother and father walked up to Ellie and Gail by the tree. They looked at Gail and did not run away.

Then Gail's mother and father walked up to the tree too. They looked at Ellie and were not afraid.

"We are sorry we ran away," said Ellie's father. "We are not used to being around a mouse, and we were afraid. But Ellie, if you can be friends with a mouse, we can too."

"And we are sorry too," said Gail's father. "If Gail can be friends with an elephant, we can too."

Ellie and Gail were so happy. "We can be friends!" shouted Ellie and Gail.

The two friends ran off to play. And from that day on, Ellie's family and Gail's family have been good friends as well.